THE CHEROKEES

BY MICHELLE LEVINE

CONSULTANT: TONIA HOGNER-WEAVEL
DIRECTOR OF EDUCATION AT THE CHEROKEE HERITAGE CENTER

LERNER PUBLICATIONS COMPANY
MINNEAPOLIS

ABOUT THE COVER IMAGE: This Cherokee snake mask is carved out of wood. Handmade masks are an important part of Cherokee culture and historical traditions.

PHOTO ACKNOWLEDGMENTS:

The photos in this book are used courtesy of: © Peabody Museum, Harvard University Photo T1201, pp. 1, 3, 4, 14, 26, 40; © Marilyn "Angel" Wynn/www.nativestock.com, pp. 5, 8, 11, 12, 13, 16, 18, 21, 22, 23, 28, 39, 46 (bottom), 47, 48, 49; © Bettmann/CORBIS, pp. 6, 34; © The Art Archive, p. 7; Tennessee State Museum Collection, p. 9; © PhotoDisc Royalty Free by Getty Images, pp. 15, 20; © AP | Wide World Photos, p. 19; © Peabody Museum, Harvard University Photo T4805, p. 24; National Anthropological Archives, Smithsonian Institution/NAA-1036, p. 25; Library of Congress, pp. 27, 30, 35, 42; © D. Ray Smith, www.Smithdray.net, p. 29; National Anthropological Archives, Smithsonian Institution/NAA-1000a, p. 31; Western History Collections, University of Oklahoma, pp. 32, 37; Courtesy of The Atlanta History Center, p. 33; © Burstein Collection/CORBIS, p. 36; © Museum of the Cherokee Indian, p. 41; © MPI/Getty Images, p. 43; Cherokee Nation of Oklahoma, p. 44; Peabody Museum, Harvard University Photo 2004.1.893, p. 45; Peabody Museum, Harvard University Photo T1228, p. 46 (top); © Sun Valley Photography/www.nativestock.com, p. 46 (middle).

Front Cover: © The Art Archive.

Lerner Publications Company
A division of Lerner Publishing Group, Inc.
241 First Avenue North
Minneapolis, MN 55401 U.S.A.

Website address: www.lernerbooks.com

Library of Congress Cataloging-in-Publication Data

Levine, Michelle.
    The Cherokees / by Michelle Levine.
      p.   cm. — (Native American histories)
    Includes bibliographical references and index.
    ISBN-13: 978-0-8225-2443-4 (lib. bdg. : alk. paper)
    ISBN-10: 0-8225-2443-0 (lib. bdg. : alk. paper)
    1. Cherokee Indians—History. 2. Cherokee Indians—Government relations.
  3. Cherokee Indians—Social life and customs. I. Title. II. Series.
  E99.C5L393 2007
  975.004'97557—dc22   2004011630

Manufactured in the United States of America
2 3 4 5 6 7 – DP – 13 12 11 10 09 08

CONTENTS

CHAPTER 1

THE CHEROKEE HOMELAND

THE CHEROKEES ARE NATIVE PEOPLE OF NORTH AMERICA.

They are often called Native Americans or American Indians. This continent is their original home. The Cherokee people have lived in North America for at least one thousand years. In early times, they lived in and around the southeastern Appalachian Mountains. At least twenty thousand Cherokee people were spread out over their large homeland. It included parts of modern-day North and South Carolina, Georgia, Alabama, Virginia, Tennessee, and Kentucky.

The Cherokee homeland was a good place to live and grow. Rich forests covered much of the area. Raccoons, wolves, mountain lions, deer, bison, and other animals roamed the forests. There were also many birds, including eagles, hawks, ravens, and wild turkeys. Fish and shellfish filled the rivers and streams.

Forests blanketed the Cherokee homeland.

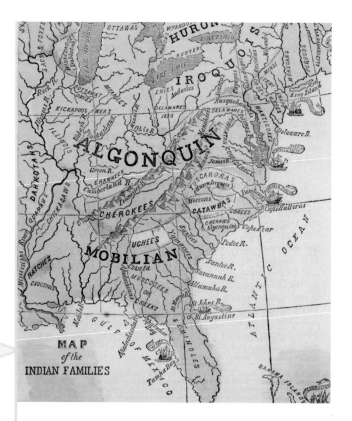

The Cherokees had many neighbors in the Southeast.

The Cherokees were not alone in the Southeast. Their homeland bordered and overlapped the land of at least nine other American Indian communities, including the Creeks, Choctaws, and Chickasaws. These groups traded with each other. At times, they also battled one another, most often over land. Different groups gave the Cherokee people different names. But the Cherokees called themselves Ani-Yun-Wiya, which means "the Real People."

EARLY LIFE

No written records exist describing the lives of the early Cherokee people. For many years, the Cherokee language was a spoken language only. Cherokee communities did not write down their words, stories, or history. But people who study Cherokee history have some ideas about the group's ancient traditions.

Making masks is a very old Cherokee tradition. Some masks are wooden like this one. Others are made out of gourds, vegetables in the squash family.

Most Cherokee families lived in permanent villages in the homeland. These villages usually stood near a river or stream. Land near water was often the best for farming. Fishing was always close by, and people could travel easily from one village to the next in canoes.

About three hundred to six hundred people lived in most villages. A village included people from the

Cherokee canoes were made from large tree trunks. Canoe makers dried the wood and then hollowed it out by carefully burning a long hole into each tree trunk.

Cherokee villages like this one were scattered throughout the Cherokee homeland's rich lands.

different Cherokee clans. People who shared the same ancestors on their mother's side belonged to the same clan. The seven Cherokee clans were Wolf, Deer, Bird, Red Paint (sometimes called Paint), Blue Paint (or Blue), Wild Potato, and Long Hair. Women played an important leadership role in each clan. Both men and women felt a strong loyalty to their clan and treated other clan members as brothers and sisters.

WOMEN WARRIORS

Women were greatly respected in the Cherokee community. Some of them were warriors and white chiefs. Women who fought in battles alongside their brothers and husbands were called Beloved Women or War Women. These women earned the right to advise village chiefs in matters of peace and war. They were also responsible for choosing punishments for people who had committed major crimes.

Each village also had its own leaders, or village chiefs, chosen by the community. The main leader was called a white chief. The white chief led religious festivals, helped keep the peace, and helped set rules for the village. Most white chiefs came from the Long Hair clan, and they were usually men. However, women may have occasionally held this position. During times of war, a red chief led a village. This war chief, who was often from the Wolf clan, organized warriors for battle and kept the village safe from enemies.

The village made important decisions together. Village members met in the village's council house to discuss public matters. The council house was a circular building. It often stood on a large mound in the center of the village. The building usually had enough seats for all the village members. People from the same clan sat together during meetings. In the center of the council house burned a sacred fire. Village leaders and warriors sat closest to this fire.

Council houses traditionally had seven sides, one for each Cherokee clan.

During a meeting, all individuals could express their opinions before a decision was made. One person spoke at a time while the rest of the group listened. Members at the meeting usually did not make a final decision until they could all agree.

After meetings, families returned to their own homes. The Cherokees built homes from wood frames plastered with grass and clay. A home usually had one door and few or no windows. An opening in the roof let out smoke from the fire.

To block wind and rain, a deer's hide usually covered the doorway of a Cherokee home.

A Cherokee hot house, called an *asi*, was used in the winter. It had very thick mud walls to hold in the fire's heat.

During the winter, families in the colder northern areas or higher in the mountains moved to a smaller home called a hot house. This small, round hut was much easier to heat.

The home was a busy place. Often grandparents, parents, and children lived together in one house. And after a daughter married, her husband came to live with her family. Children were mainly raised by their mother, grandmother, aunts, and older sisters. Uncles, grandfathers, and other male relatives also helped children learn and grow. Family was the center of a Cherokee child's life.

CHAPTER 2

DAILY LIFE

MOST CHEROKEES LIVED BY COMMON RELIGIOUS AND SPIRITUAL BELIEFS. They believed that nature was more powerful than humans were. Everything from animals to rivers and mountains should be respected. Legends about the natural world were passed down from generation to generation.

According to one traditional legend, the Cherokee people believed that Earth was an island in a huge body of water. The island was attached to the sky by a strong cord at each of the four corners. The sky itself was a great vault, or dome, made of rock.

Many Cherokee legends explain why animals and other parts of nature are the way they are.

One traditional Cherokee tale tells how the deer got his antlers. The story says that he won them in a contest with the rabbit.

This storyteller works at the Cherokee Heritage Center in Tahlequah, Oklahoma. He keeps ancient tales alive by sharing them with modern Cherokees.

Some of these stories also taught the Cherokees how to live. These stories showed how a person's good or bad actions led to good or bad fortune. Yet at times, problems such as an illness or failure in battle seemed to occur without a reason. When this happened, a person might seek the help of a medicine man. This spiritual healer would perform special rituals and make medicine from plants to cure an illness or to take away bad luck.

THE CREATION OF EARTH

The Cherokees tell many different stories to explain how Earth was created. One well-known story says that in the beginning there was no Earth, only the sea. And there were no people. The animals lived in the sky vault made of rock. But the sky became too crowded. One day, Water Beetle decided to explore the sea. First, he explored the top of water. Then he dove down beneath the sea to its muddy bottom. He swam back up with some soft mud. The mud spread on the water and became the island of Earth. After that, all the animals came down to live on Earth. But it was too dark to see anything. The animals directed the sun to move across the sky from east to west. Then man and woman were created. The first man was called Kanati, and the first woman was Selu.

The fire that burns inside the council house is very special. It represents Cherokee religious beliefs, as well as the unity of the Cherokee people.

Inside the council house, a new sacred fire was lit for the year. The village forgave all crimes. Neighbors and friends also forgave each other for arguments or harmful actions.

The Cherokees also came together to celebrate other special events. The Victory Dance occurred after warriors returned from a successful battle with another Native American community.

The Animal Dance took place before a great hunt to bring good luck to the hunters. The Ball Play Dance occurred before a match of stickball, a popular Cherokee game.

FARMING, HUNTING, AND OTHER CHORES

Between festivals and celebrations, Cherokee people kept busy with farming, fishing, and hunting.

Cherokee farmers used many tools, such as this hoe made from wood and stone.

Farming fields sat on the outer edges of each village. Men, women, and children worked together to dig up the soil each spring and to plant crops such as corn, beans, pumpkins, and sunflowers. After planting, women tended the fields and harvested most of the crops. Women also gathered wild fruits, vegetables, and herbs in the forests. Some of the herbs were used as medicine for illnesses.

This basket holds squash, beans, nuts, and other important Cherokee crops.

When a Cherokee hunter blew into one end of a blowgun, a dart shot out the other end. Part of the thistle flower was used on the end of the dart to help it fly straight.

Cherokee men were responsible for fishing and hunting. Fishers used bows and arrows, underwater traps, spears, and baited hooks to catch many kinds of fish. Carefully trained hunters worked together to capture large animals. They used the bow and arrow to kill animals such as deer, bears, bison, and turkeys. They used blowguns with sharp wooden darts to kill smaller animals, such as rabbits and birds.

The hunters and fishers brought their catches home to their families. Women used many parts of the animals for clothing and food.

Women turned fur into warm blankets and winter outfits. They made animal skins into clothing, including shirts, dresses, robes, and moccasins. They sewed this clothing using needles made of fish bone. Other animal bones became knives or pieces of jewelry.

The animals killed by hunters also provided food for families. Women roasted, fried, or boiled the animal meat. They also baked different kinds of bread, cooked soups, and prepared drinks. They cooked over a fire using pots and utensils they had made out of clay.

Cherokees used wood to make tools such as this comb.

Cherokee pottery is both attractive and useful.

Along with farming, hunting, and fishing, there were other important chores. Women wove baskets and made pottery. They gathered wood for fires and carried drinking water from rivers and streams. Men repaired homes, dug out new canoes, and made new blowguns, bows, and arrows.

In the winter months, warriors fought battles with neighboring American Indian communities. Many wars occurred over land boundaries. The Cherokees also fought wars of revenge when other groups raided Cherokee villages.

CHAPTER 3

DIFFICULT YEARS

IN 1540, EUROPEANS ENTERED CHEROKEE LAND FOR THE FIRST TIME. Led by Hernando de Soto, a group of Spanish explorers had a brief and peaceful encounter with the Cherokees. Later, during the 1600s, more and more Europeans began arriving in North America. Many came to hunt animals for their valuable fur. They traded cloth, shoes, weapons, tools, and other useful items for fur from Cherokee hunters.

Hernando de Soto was one of the first Europeans to set foot in the Cherokee homeland. He was searching for gold and other precious resources.

The Cherokees soon realized that Europeans wanted more than fur. They also wanted land. Without permission, British settlers began forming colonies on the Cherokee homeland. For a while, these colonists and the Cherokees mostly got along with each other. But the Cherokee people were unhappy about losing some of their land.

Then, in the 1730s, the Cherokees lost much more than their land. Many of them lost their lives.

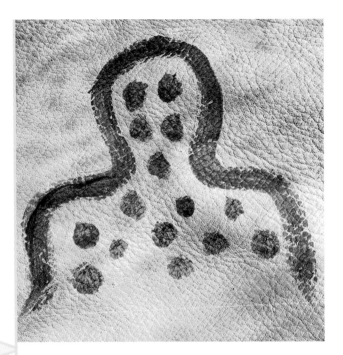

Smallpox killed hundreds of Cherokees and other Native Americans. Painted symbols such as this one warned people to stay away from places where the disease had struck.

Smallpox, a deadly disease brought from Europe, swept through one Cherokee village after another. Smallpox may have killed up to half of the Cherokee population. The loss of so many people was a great tragedy for the Cherokees.

A NEW NATION

In 1783, the people of the British colonies won the Revolutionary War (1775–1783) against Great Britain. The colonists declared themselves independent and formed the United States of

America. Like the British rulers, the new U.S. government wanted to take Cherokee land for its citizens.

In 1785, Cherokee leaders met with U.S. leaders to sign a written agreement called the Treaty of Hopewell. The most powerful Cherokee chief at the meeting was Corn Tassel. He spoke for his people, saying, "We shall be satisfied if we are paid for the lands we have given up, but we will not, nor cannot, give up any more land."

NANCY WARD was a famous Beloved Woman in the late 1700s. She was both a skillful warrior and a respected leader. She also believed in trying to make peace with white people. In 1785, she took part in the Treaty of Hopewell talks between Cherokee leaders and the U.S government.

George Washington became the first U.S. president in 1789. Cherokee leaders asked him and the U.S. Congress to honor the Treaty of Hopewell.

The Treaty of Hopewell set up the boundaries between Cherokee land and U.S. land. The U.S. leaders promised that no more white people would settle on Cherokee territory. But this promise was quickly broken. White settlers continued to live on Cherokee land without permission. Some Cherokees fought these settlers. Others thought that fighting could not solve the problem. They wanted to make peace. But over time, many Cherokees came to believe that neither fighting nor peacemaking would save their land.

CHANGING CHEROKEE LIFE

Life with white neighbors changed the Cherokee people. Many Cherokees began living in log cabins instead of traditional homes. Instead of growing crops together, they planted on their own farms using tools and methods brought from Europe. Instead of using animal skins and fur, many women spun clothing out of wool and cotton. Some people married white settlers and sometimes raised children who could speak, read, and write English.

Some Cherokee customs faded when white settlers arrived. These women stand outside a log cabin and wear clothes like those of the settlers.

FACSIMILE OF CHEROKEE ALPHABET BEFORE PRINTING.

ᏒᎠᎳᎳᎬᏋᏊᏃᏈᎯᏈᏔᎡᏈᏔᏉᎥᏀᎻᏟᏲᏔᏀᏔᏯ

1 A, short. 2 A broad. 3 Lah. 4 Tsee. 5 Nah. 6 Weeh. 7 Weh. 8 Leeh. 9 Neh. 10 Mooh. 11 Keeh 12 Yeeh. 13 Seeh. 14 Clanh. 15 Ah. 16 Luh. 17 Leh. 18 Hah. 19 Woh. 20 Cloh. 21 Tah. 22 Yahn. 23 Lahn. 24 Hee. 25 Ss (sibilant.) 26 Yoh. Un (French.) 28 Hoo. 29 Goh. 30 Tsoo. 31 Maugh. 32 Seh. 33 Saugh. 34 Cleegh. 35 Queegh. 36 Quegh. 37 Sah. 38 Quah. 39 Gnaugh (nasal.) 40 Kaah. 41 Tsahn 42 Sahn. 43 Neeh. 44 Kah. 45 Taugh. 46 Keh. 47 Taah. 48 Khan. 49 Weeh. 50 Eeh. 51 Ooh. 52 Yeh. 53 Un. 54 Tun. 55 Kooh. 56 Tsoh. 57 Quoh. 58 Noo. 59 Na. 60 Loh. 61. Yu. 62 Tseh. 63 Tee. 64 Wahn. 65 Tooh. 66 Teh. 67 Tsah. 68 Un. 69 Neh. 70 ―― 71 Tsooh. 72 Mah. 73 Clooh. 74 Haah. 75 Hah. 76 Meeh. 77 Clah. 78 Yah. 79 Wah. 80 Teeh. 81 Clegh. 82 Naa. 83 Quh. 84 Clah. 85 Maah 86 Quhn.

Sequoyah's alphabet uses eighty-six different symbols. Each symbol represents a sound in the Cherokee language.

Cherokees became successful farmers, landowners, and business owners. They learned to live in both Cherokee and white society. Yet with all these changes came a great loss. As the oldest Cherokees died, some of the group's traditions were forgotten.

READING, WRITING, AND GOVERNMENT

In 1821, a Cherokee leader named Sequoyah invented an alphabet so that his people could read and write in their language. This invention paved the way for many more changes. It allowed the Cherokees to set up schools and to publish the first Cherokee newspaper, the *Cherokee Phoenix*.

Sequoyah's invention also helped the Cherokee people take part in their government. By the early 1800s, Cherokee leaders had formed a single, central government to represent all of their people.

SEQUOYAH was probably born in the 1760s in the Cherokee village of Tuskegee in modern-day Tennessee. The Cherokee alphabet that he invented in 1821 quickly spread from one Cherokee village to the next. It allowed thousands of Cherokee people to read and write for the first time.

Eventually, Sequoyah's alphabet would be used on the seal of the Cherokee Nation, a symbol of the group's new government.

They chose one principal chief to lead the government. They set up a capital, called New Echota, for what became known as the Cherokee Nation. They also created a court system, as well as a legislature to make the nation's laws.

Using Sequoyah's new alphabet, Cherokee officials wrote down the government's constitution. This set of laws was published in the first issue of the *Cherokee Phoenix* for all Cherokees to read. After that, new Cherokee laws and important decisions were recorded in writing and helped unite the Cherokee community.

In many ways, the Cherokee people were thriving. But they still had one big problem. White settlers continued to take more and more land for themselves. Sometimes they forced Cherokee families out of their homes. Finally, Cherokee leaders asked U.S. president Andrew Jackson for help. Years earlier, Cherokee fighters had helped President Jackson win a war against the Creek Indians. The Cherokees hoped he would return the favor.

Andrew Jackson, a former army general, was called Old Hickory by his soldiers. His nickname among Cherokee people was Sharp Knife.

Not everyone in the U.S. government supported the Indian Removal Act. Congressman Davy Crockett of Tennessee, for instance, was fiercely opposed to the law.

But Jackson sided with the settlers. In 1830, he signed the Indian Removal Act. This law said that all American Indians must leave their land and move to land west of the Mississippi River.

The Cherokee people refused to give in without a fight. They took their case to the highest court in the United States, the Supreme Court, and won. But the U.S. government still told them they had to move west.

THE TRAIL OF TEARS

In 1838, troops of the U.S. Army arrived in the Southeast to force the Cherokees off their land. Soldiers barged into Cherokee homes and demanded that families leave immediately. People barely had time to pack up a few belongings. They left behind furniture, farm animals, and tools. Most painful of all was the loss of their homeland, where their ancestors had lived for generations.

JOHN ROSS became the first principal chief of the Cherokee people in 1828. Ross did everything he could to keep Cherokees on their homeland. But eventually he was forced to move. He was the leader of the new Cherokee Nation in the Indian Territory until his death in 1866.

THE FIVE CIVILIZED TRIBES

In the mid-1800s, the Cherokees became known as one of the Five Civilized Tribes in the United States. The other four groups, sometimes called tribes, were the Chickasaws, Creeks, Seminoles, and Choctaws. White Americans used this term as praise. They believed that these five groups fit in best with white society and were therefore the most "civilized." Many Americans did not understand or respect traditional Indian cultures. Eventually, all five tribes elected their own principal leaders. They created their own constitutions, court systems, legislatures, and public school systems.

Men, women, and children were herded like animals into small and dirty prison camps. Deadly illnesses spread easily in the camps. The Cherokees were not cared for or given enough to eat. Many people died.

When fall came, soldiers forced the Indians to march one thousand miles westward to the Indian

Territory. The Indian Territory was an area in modern-day Oklahoma. The U.S. government had set aside this land for Native Americans to live on.

As the Cherokees traveled westward, they did not have proper food or winter clothing. Many more people died. In all, at least four thousand Cherokee people lost their lives on the difficult journey. The Cherokees called this terrible time the Trail of Tears.

The Trail of Tears brought suffering to the Cherokee people. Even worse, it forced them to leave their homeland.

CHAPTER 4

BUILDING A NEW LIFE

THE CHEROKEE PEOPLE TRIED TO MAKE THE BEST OF THEIR NEW HOME IN THE INDIAN TERRITORY.

In 1839, they wrote a new constitution for their government. For the next twenty years, the Cherokee Nation worked hard to rebuild a good life for its people. Cherokee leaders set up a new legislature, a court system, a jail, public schools, and a newspaper. Families started farms, ranches, and businesses. They built new homes and formed close communities.

But life kept twisting and turning. In 1861, the country's Northern and Southern states went to war against each other in the Civil War. The war was fought, in part, over the issue of slavery.

Slavery had been outlawed in the North. It was still important to farms and other businesses in the South. Most members of the Cherokee Nation sided with the North during the war, but some Cherokees fought for the South.

These Cherokee men were soldiers in the Southern army during the Civil War. They hold the flag of the Confederate South.

Tensions over this difference within the Cherokee Nation weakened the community. The war itself destroyed many homes, buildings, and farms on Cherokee land.

After the war ended in 1865, the U.S. government began chipping away at the Indian Territory. They gave some Cherokee land to other American Indian groups who had been forced from

This political cartoon shows the Cherokee people being mistreated by the white settlers.

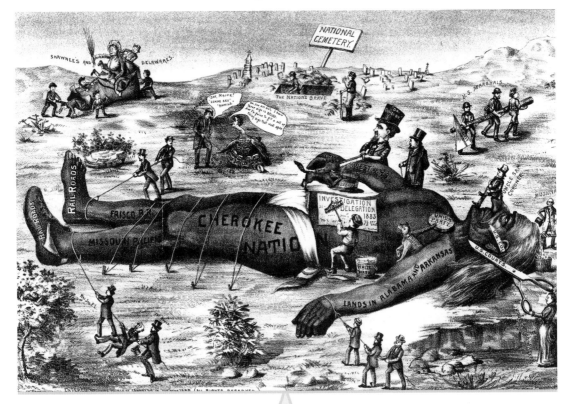

White settlers rushed to build homes and businesses on land that had once been the Cherokee homeland.

their homes. Other land was split apart by new railroads that cut across Cherokee communities.

Matters grew worse in 1907. That year, the Indian Territory became part of the new state of Oklahoma. The U.S. government took apart the Cherokee government and took away the power of the principal chief. And Cherokee families continued to lose their land to white farmers and ranchers.

Still, the Cherokee people worked to improve their lives and their community. In 1961, the U.S. government paid them for some of the land they had lost. And in the 1970s, the Cherokee Nation regained the right to run its own government and live by its own laws. Throughout the end of the 1900s and into the 2000s, the Cherokee Nation grew stronger and stronger.

WILMA MANKILLER was the first woman to be elected principal chief of the Cherokee Nation. She held this office from 1985 to 1995 and became one of the most popular and outspoken Cherokee leaders.

Maude Welch is a Cherokee artist who helps keep alive the Cherokee tradition of pottery making.

THE CHEROKEES IN MODERN TIMES

More than 200,000 people are members of the modern Cherokee Nation. It is the second-largest Indian community in the country. More than half of these Cherokees live in Oklahoma.

Some Cherokee families live in towns with many white neighbors. Others live in traditional communities similar to the Cherokee villages of long ago. Cherokee men and women make their living in a variety of ways. They are salespeople, construction workers, business owners, teachers, artists, farmers, and other workers.

STICKBALL: A CONTINUING CHEROKEE TRADITION

In ancient times, Cherokee men played a game called A-ne-jo-di, or stickball. Every player held a wooden stick with stiff netting at one end. Players on two teams used these sticks to toss a ball as close as possible to the top of a tall goalpost.

At times, the game was played to settle arguments between rival towns or groups of people. Before each game, the players performed a ceremonial dance. One woman from each of the seven clans also took part in the dance. The Cherokees still play A-ne-jo-di. Both men and women take part in the modern games.

Stickball players, both in the past (*above*) and today (*right*) use the traditional wooden stick (*top*) to catch and throw the ball.

This guide works at the Oconaluftee Indian Village
in Cherokee, North Carolina.

Some Cherokees live in parts of the original
homeland in the Southeast. In North Carolina, a
community called the Eastern Band of Cherokee
Indians lives on a reservation—land set aside for
American Indians by the U.S. government. The
Eastern Band has more than twelve thousand
members. It has its own government and principal
chief. The Cherokees of Georgia, a smaller group,
live on the original Cherokee homeland.
Cherokee people also live in cities and towns
across the United States.

Throughout the year, Cherokee men, women, and children still come together for traditional festivals and ceremonies. Religious dances called stomp dances are regularly held outdoors. A sacred fire is lit and kept burning for the entire event. During the day, Cherokee leaders give religious talks. After sundown, the first ceremonial dance begins. Later, people visit, feast, and dance all through the night.

This Cherokee girl has won the Junior Miss Cherokee Pageant, a modern community event. Winning contestants must know a lot about Cherokee history and culture.

Cherokee people also gather for many other cultural events. For example, the annual Cherokee National Holiday honors the signing of the 1839 Cherokee constitution. Another popular event is the performance of a play telling the story of the Trail of Tears. This drama is shown every year in Tahlequah, Oklahoma, the capital of the Cherokee Nation. The Cherokee Heritage Center in Tahlequah also holds special events, including storytelling festivals and art shows.

Visitors to New Echota, Georgia, can see a re-creation of the *Cherokee Phoenix* offices. The *Phoenix* was the first newspaper written in the Cherokee language.

The Eastern Band of Cherokee Indians hosts its own cultural attractions. Events include a yearly performance of the Cherokee play *Unto These Hills*.

Over the years, the Cherokee people have shown that they are strong survivors. They take pride in the traditions of the past and weave them into their lives. And as they have done for centuries, the Cherokees continue to grow, change, and look toward the future.

BEAN BREAD

This traditional recipe uses beans and corn, crops grown by the early Cherokee people.

> 1 cup cornmeal
> ½ cup all-purpose flour
> 2 teaspoons baking powder
> 1 tablespoon sugar
> ¼ cup vegetable shortening
> 1 egg
> 2 cups milk
> 2 tablespoons honey
> 4 cups canned beans (pinto or red), drained

1. Preheat oven to 450°F.
2. Mix together cornmeal, flour, baking powder, and sugar.
3. Melt shortening in a microwave or in a small saucepan over medium heat. Remove from heat and let cool.
4. Beat egg in a small bowl.
5. Add milk, melted shortening, beaten egg, and honey to the dry ingredients. Stir until smooth. Add beans and use a gentle, overturning motion to mix together.
6. Pour batter into a greased loaf pan. Bake for about 30 minutes, or until golden brown.

Makes 1 loaf

PLACES TO VISIT

Cherokee Heritage Center

Tahlequah, Oklahoma

(918) 456-6007

http://www.cherokeeheritage.org/

This is the main cultural center for the Cherokee Nation in Oklahoma. The center includes the Tsa-La-Gi outdoor amphitheater, the Tsa-La-Gi Ancient Village, Adams Corner Rural Village and Farm, and the Cherokee National Museum. The center also hosts yearly cultural events.

The Museum of the Cherokee Indian

Cherokee, North Carolina

(828) 497-3481

http://www.cherokeemuseum.org/

This museum is run by the Eastern Band of Cherokee Indians. It includes many exhibits and collections that explore the history and traditions of Cherokee Indians in North America.

Oconaluftee Indian Village

Cherokee, North Carolina

(828) 497-2315

http://www.oconalufteevillage.com

Run by the Cherokee Historical Association in North Carolina, this living history museum takes visitors back in time to a Cherokee village of the past.

Sequoyah Birthplace Museum

Vonore, Tennessee

(423) 884-6246

http://www.sequoyahmuseum.org

Located in the Smoky Mountains of eastern Tennessee, this museum honors Sequoyah, the inventor of the Cherokee alphabet.

GLOSSARY

asi: a Cherokee family's winter home. An asi was also called a hot house.

Beloved Woman: a woman who fought in battle alongside her brothers and husband. Beloved Women were also called "War Women."

chief: a Cherokee leader. Traditionally, each Cherokee village had a white chief for peacetime and a red chief for wartime. Later, the Cherokee Nation chose one principal chief.

clan: a large group of families sharing a common ancestor on the mother's side. Traditional Cherokee society was divided into seven clans.

council house: a Cherokee village's meeting place. Council houses were traditionally large circular buildings. They stood in the center of each village.

legislature: the group that makes a government's laws

native: originally from a place. The Cherokee are native to North America.

reservation: land set aside for American Indians by the U.S. government. Most Indians were forced off their homeland and onto reservations in the 1800s.

Supreme Court: the highest court in the United States

treaty: a written agreement

FURTHER READING

Bealer, Alex W. *Only the Names Remain: The Cherokees and the Trail of Tears.* Boston: Little, Brown, 1996. This book describes the difficult journey that Cherokees were forced to make from their homeland to the Indian Territory in modern-day Oklahoma.

Dadey, Debbie. *Cherokee Sister*. New York: Delacorte Press, 2000. A white girl becomes friends with a Cherokee girl and is accidentally swept from her home in the Trail of Tears.

Duvall, Deborah. *The Great Ball Game of the Birds and Animals*. Albuquerque: University of New Mexico Press, 2002. This is the tale of a game of stickball between the earth's large and small animals.

Flanagan, Alice K. *Mrs. Scott's Beautiful Art*. New York. Children's Press, 1999. This book describes the work of a Cherokee artist who uses many natural materials to create art in the tradition of her ancestors.

Lowery, Linda. *Wilma Mankiller*. Minneapolis: Carolrhoda Books, Inc., 1996. This is a biography of the first woman to become principal chief of the modern Cherokee Nation.

Pennington, Daniel. *Itse Selu: Cherokee Harvest Festival*. Watertown, MA: Charlesbridge, 1994. In this story, a young Cherokee boy celebrates Itse Selu, the Green Corn Festival.

Roop, Peter, and Connie Roop. *If You Lived with the Cherokee*. New York: Scholastic, 1998. This book describes what life was like for Cherokee children and adults long ago.

Waxman, Laura Hamilton. *Sequoyah*. Minneapolis: Lerner Publications Company, 2005. This biography is of the inventor of the Cherokee alphabet.

WEBSITES

Cherokee Indians of Georgia
http://cherokee-indians-of-ga-inc.0pi.com/
This website includes information about this community's traditions and government.

Official Homepage of the Eastern Band of Cherokee Indians
http://www.cherokee-nc.com/
This site provides information about Eastern Cherokees and the many visitor attractions on the reservation.

Official Website of the Cherokee Nation
http://www.cherokee.org/
This large website has many helpful links to information about the Cherokee Nation and the Cherokee culture, including a "Kids Corner."

SELECTED BIBLIOGRAPHY

French, Laurence, and Jim Hornbuckle, eds. *The Cherokee Perspective: Written by Eastern Cherokee*. Boone, NC: Appalachian Consortium Press, 1981.

Hoig, Stan. *The Cherokees and Their Chiefs: In the Wake of Empire*. Fayetteville: University of Arkansas Press, 1998.

Mails, Thomas E. *The Cherokee People: The Story of the Cherokees from Earliest Origins to Contemporary Times*. Tulsa, OK: Council Oak Books, 1992.

Mankiller, Wilma, and Michael Wallis. *Mankiller: A Chief and Her People*. New York: St. Martin's Press, 1993.

Rozema, Vicki. *Cherokee Voices: Early Accounts of Cherokee Life in the East*. Winston-Salem, NC: John F. Blair, 2002.

Sturm, Circe. *Blood Politics: Race, Culture, and Identity in the Cherokee Nation of Oklahoma*. Berkeley: University of California Press, 2002.

Wallace. Anthony F. C. *The Long, Bitter Trail: Andrew Jackson and the Indians*. New York: Hill and Wang, 1993.

INDEX